Ganny Says

**Wisdom from First Lady Barbara Bush,
America's Grandmother**

CHRIS HELENE BRIDGE

Foreword by
Lauren Bush Lauren

 bright sky publishing
HOUSTON, TEXAS

All Ganny Says quotes are by Barbara Bush

Bright Sky Publishing
2365 Rice Blvd., Suite 202 │ Houston, Texas 77005

ISBN: 978-1-942945-78-9

10 9 8 7 6 5 4 3 2 1

Library of Congress Cataloging-in-Publication Data on file with the publisher.

Editorial Director: Lucy Herring Chambers │ Editor: Aries Jones │ Designer: Marla Y. Garcia │ Printed in Canada through Friesens

• FOREWORD •

"Eat your veggies, and sit up straight. Tell the truth, and don't be late." These words of wisdom and many others are how I remember my Ganny. She never shied away from sharing her advice and guidance, especially with us grandkids. During my childhood, there was no getting behind or around Ganny, as she magically seemed to see and know everything. To know and love Ganny was to respect her, and now her instructive lessons are etched into my memory and into my life. Through this book, I look forward to sharing some of my Ganny's wisdom with my boys, James and Max, as well as her love of reading!

– Lauren Bush Lauren

"When you read to your child,
put your arms around them
and they will feel loved and secure."

– First Lady Barbara Bush –

Ganny was a grandma,
and our First Lady, too.
Ganny was strong and wise,
and knew just what to do.

This is what she told her kids,
then told her grandkids, too:

"To make this world a better place
begins with me and you."

Why do you think it is important to listen to a person who is wise?

Did You Know?
Mrs. Bush believed that everyone should do their part and that good manners are important. She made a list of rules for her children and grandchildren to follow when they came to visit their home each summer in Kennebunkport, Maine, and posted them in each of their bedrooms.

Ganny Says:
"At the end of your life... you will never regret not having passed a test, not winning one more verdict or not closing one more deal. You will regret time not spent with a husband, a friend, a child or a parent."

So come along and listen
to some things that Ganny knows.
And give your full attention,
because what Ganny says, goes!

"Say please and thank you and don't be shy.
Look at others in the eye."

What can you do to make sure you get somewhere on time?

Did You Know?
Mrs. Bush was called Ganny by her grandchildren. Ganny's grandchildren knew, without a doubt, that when Ganny told them to do something, she meant it! Ganny was also known as "The Enforcer."

Ganny Says:
"Study hard, work hard and play hard too."

"Eat your veggies, and sit up straight. Tell the truth, and don't be late."

Have you ever been angry with yourself when you made a mistake? Have you ever laughed at yourself instead of being angry? How did it feel?

Did You Know?

Ganny tried to laugh at her troubles and not take things too seriously. One of the ways she did this was by wearing Keds sneakers that didn't match and waiting for someone to notice!

Ganny Says:

"Don't cry over things that were or things that aren't. Enjoy what you have now to the fullest."

"Laugh at yourself. Make others laugh, too. They'll feel better, and so will you!"

Ganny's favorite book was called Pride and Prejudice. *What is your favorite book? Why?*

Did You Know?
Ganny enjoyed tennis, golf and swimming. She decided to not worry too much about growing older or coloring her hair. Instead, she enjoyed spending time with her family and friends and read many great books!

Ganny Says:
"Everything I am concerned about would be better if more people could read, write and comprehend."

"Don't think too much about your looks. Spend more time reading books!"

"Learn to count and write and read. This will help with every need."

What do you enjoy doing? How can you use your talents and interests to help others?

Did You Know?
Making a better world for future generations was important to Ganny. One day she was planting some peonies in her garden in Maine. Peonies were her favorite flower, but she said she was planting them for her children and grandchildren because they would be blooming long after she was gone. Ganny also believed in writing handwritten notes of appreciation and encouragement to people and putting books into the hands of those in need.

Ganny Says:
"When you come to a roadblock, take a detour."

"Refuse to complain or say things that are bad.
It just makes things worse or someone sad."

"What helps most is doing your part.
Share your talents and your heart."

"Make a difference; use your voice.
Send a letter, you have a choice!"

*It takes practice
to become good at
something. What are
you practicing to
improve your skills?*

Did You Know?

Neil, one of Ganny's sons,
was dyslexic, so reading was
very hard for him. Some
thought he would never be
able to read, but day after
day Ganny helped Neil
practice. They never gave up.
Finally, he learned to read!

Ganny Says:

"You don't just luck into
things as much as you
would like to think you
do. You build step by step,
whether it's friendships
or opportunities."

"Take a step; then, take a few more.
Soon you'll be running, then you will soar!"

Can you think of someone you know who needs some help or encouragement?

Did You Know?
Ganny believed that everyone had value and all should be treated with respect. She never looked down on anyone.

Ganny Says:
"Never lose sight of the fact that the most important yardstick of your success will be how you treat other people—your family, friends and coworkers, and even strangers you meet along the way."

"Lift others up when they are down. Spread love and kindness all around."

What are you thankful for?

Did You Know?
Ganny believed in the power of prayer and loved God with all her heart and soul.

Ganny Says:
"You may think the president is all-powerful, but he is not. He needs a lot of guidance from the Lord."

"Be glad and thankful every day. Things work out when you pause and pray!"

Has someone ever held your hand or just sat beside you when you were alone? Did it make you feel better?

Did You Know?

Ganny thought loving her family was her most important job. She held hands with her husband as long as she lived.

Ganny Says:

"I think togetherness is a very important ingredient of family life. To us, family means putting your arms around each other and being there."

"It's the little things that mean so much; as simple as a gentle touch."

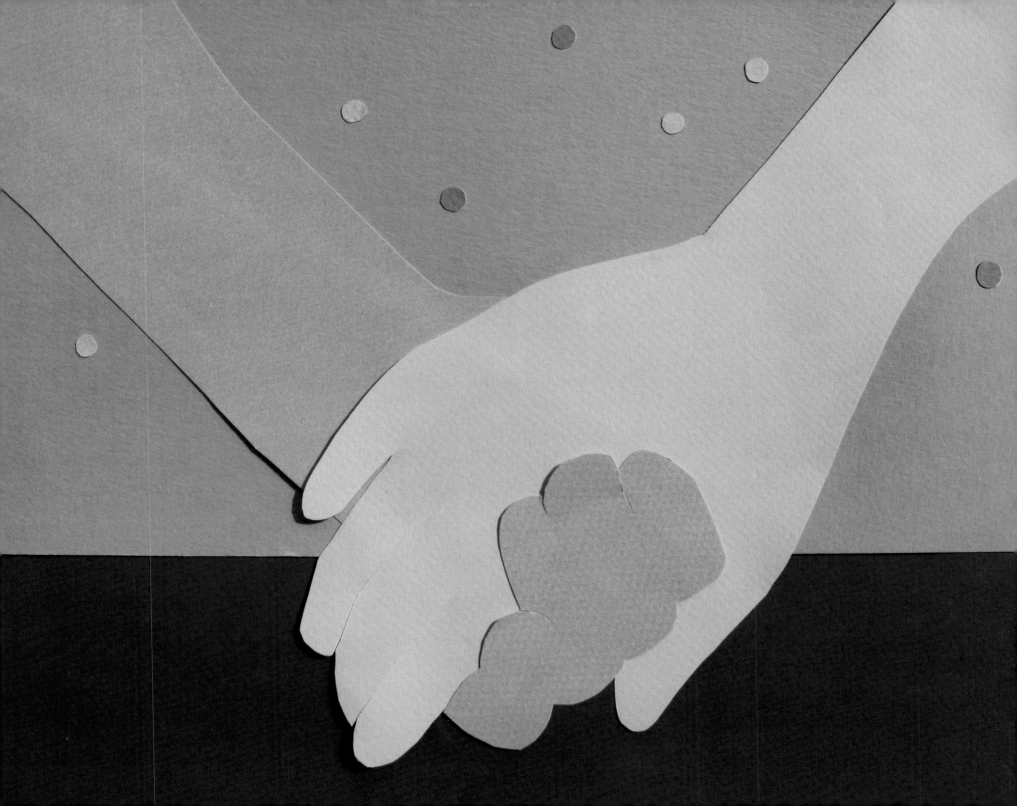

Did You Know?

Points of Light is the world's largest organization dedicated to volunteer service. It was inspired by Ganny's husband, President George H.W. Bush, as he spoke in his inaugural address about 1000 points of light. Today, Points of Light supports millions of volunteers worldwide.

Ganny Says:

"Giving frees us from the familiar territory of our own needs by opening our mind to the unexplained worlds occupied by the needs of others."

"We all can shine like a star so bright!
We all can be a point of light!"

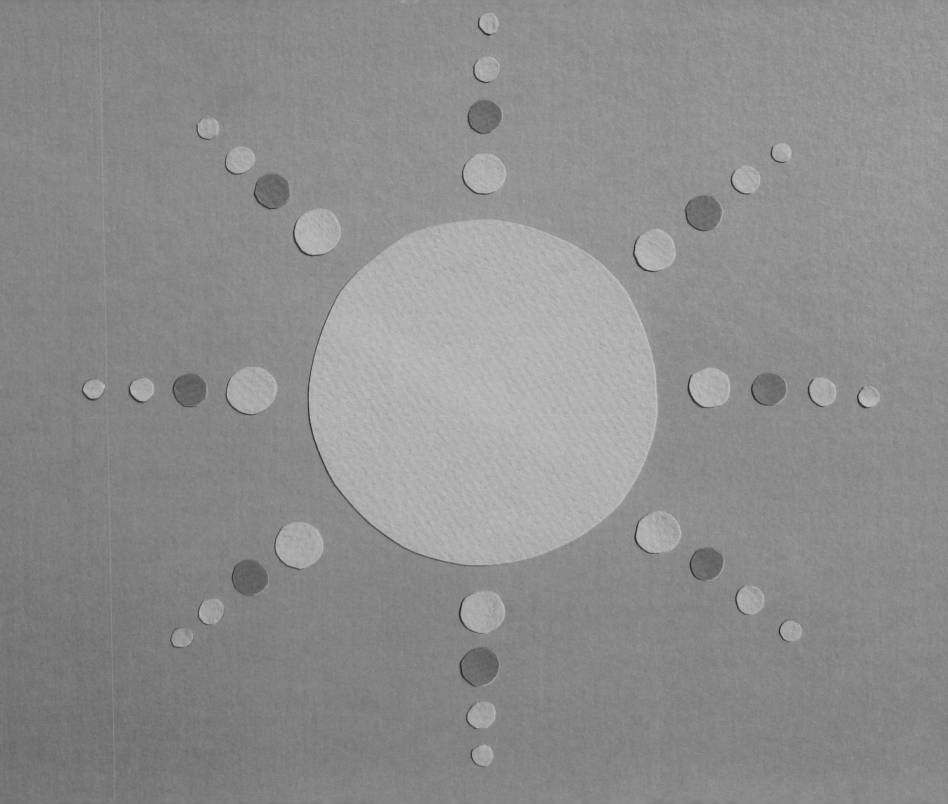

How can you be helpful throughout your day?

Did You Know?
Ganny said that words matter, kindness matters and that we are here to help each other for as long as possible.

Ganny Says:
"Believe in something larger than yourself...get involved in the big ideas of your time."

"Ganny says, and we will, too, this is just what we will do!"

"We will grow up kind and strong, helping others as we go along."

Did you know that smiles are contagious? When you smile at someone they will probably smile, too. Try it!

Did You Know?
Ganny believed that everyone has something to give. Some people give their time, some give their money, and some give their skills and connections. There is joy in both giving and receiving.

Ganny Says:
"Whether you are talking about education, career or service, you are talking about life. And life must really have joy. It's supposed to be fun."

"This world will become a better place, and we'll see smiles on every face!"

When you show your love to someone, it makes everyone around you feel good! Our love reaches farther than we can imagine and makes a bigger difference than we know! Who will you share your love with today?

Did You Know?
Ganny loved people and thought that loving each other was the most important thing of all.

Ganny Says:
"I love you more than tongue can tell."

Now you know what Ganny says.
Remember that it's true.

"To make this world a better place, begins with love from me and you!"

• GANNY'S RULES •

1. Say please and thank you when you need or receive something.
2. Ask whoever is caring for you what you can do to help.
3. Smile and have a positive attitude.
4. Please hang up your damp towels and use twice if possible.
5. Try to make your beds and keep your room picked up.
6. Collect your things around the house; keep them in your room.
7. Come to eat on time and help clear the table after eating.
8. Please put your dirty clothes where they belong.
9. Remember to share what you have.
10. Wait your turn to speak. Say "excuse me" if you need to get some attention right away.
11. Compliment others and speak kindly.
12. Ask questions to get to know others better.
13. Everyone makes mistakes; remember to apologize.
14. Introduce yourself on the phone so others know who is calling.
15. Have fun, help others and do your best!

"Treat others the way
you want to be treated."

– First Lady Barbara Bush –